Science & Religion: The Battle for the Human Mind

Dr. Shashi Bhushan

"It Is The Fundamental Duty Of Every Citizen To Develop A Scientific Temper, Humanism, And The Spirit Of Inquiry And Reform."

Article 51A, Constitution of India

Dedication

To my loving parents,

This book is a humble tribute to your unwavering support and care. Your encouragement, wisdom, and sacrifices have made me who I am today. I will always be thankful for your love and guidance.

Dr. Shashi Bhushan

CONTENT

Chapter	Title	Page no.
Chapter I	**Foundations of Science and Religion**	**1-33**
1.1	*Defining Science and Religion:*	*1*
1.1.1	*Science: Empirical inquiry, skepticism, and the pursuit of evidence-based knowledge*	*1*
1.1.2	*Religion: Faith, spirituality, and the search for meaning beyond the material world*	*5*
1.1.3	*Historical context of the science-religion debate.*	*9*
1.2	*Historical Perspectives*	*13*
1.2.1	*Ancient Civilizations: Science and Religion as Intertwined*	*13*
1.2.2	*Mesopotamia: Astronomy, Mathematics, and Divine Will*	*13*
1.2.3	*Egypt: Engineering, Medicine, and Spiritual Significance*	*14*
1.2.4	*India: Buddhism, Ayurveda, and Scientific Inquiry*	*15*
1.2.5	*China: Daoism, Confucianism, and the Natural World*	*16*
1.2.6	*Greece: Philosophical Rationalism and Mysticism*	*17*
1.3	*The Enlightenment: The Rise of Scientific Reasoning and Its Challenge to Religious Dogma*	*21*
1.3.1	*The Monk Who Brought Order to Nature*	*23*
1.3.2	*A Legacy of Reason and Discovery*	*25*
1.4	*Modern Era: The Ongoing Tension and Dialogue Between Science and Religion*	*27*
1.4.1	*A Trial That Shook the World*	*27*
1.4.2	*The Expanding Universe and the Mind of God*	*28*

1..4.3	*Mendel's Pea Plants: A Monk's Contribution to Science*	*29*
1.4.4	*The Medical Revolution: Miracles and Ethics*	*29*
1.4.5	*Climate Change: A Call for Unity?*	*30*
1.4.6	*Artificial Intelligence and the Future of Faith*	*31*
1.4.7	*A Dialogue That Never Ends*	*32*
Chapter II	**Cognitive Development and Worldview Formation**	**35-55**
2.1	*The Role of Science in Mental Development*	*35*
2.1.1	*Critical Thinking and Problem-Solving Skills*	*36*
2.1.2	*Encouraging Curiosity and Skepticism*	*37*
2.1.3	*The Impact of Scientific Literacy on Decision-Making and Worldview*	*38*
2.2	*The Role of Religion in Mental Development*	*42*
2.2.1	*Conformity and Resistance to New Ideas*	*43*
2.2.2	*Luck, and Resistance to Change*	*44*
2.2.3	*Challenges of Critical Thinking*	*45*
2.3	*Comparative Analysis between Science and Religion*	*48*
2.3.1	*Science and Rational Thinking*	*48*
2.3.2	*Religion and Faith-Based Thinking*	*49*
2.4	*The Potential Conflicts and Synergies Between Empirical Reasoning and Faith-Based Beliefs*	*50*
2.4.1	*Conflicts Between Science and Religion*	*50*
2.4.2	*Synergies Between Science and Religion*	*51*
2.4.3	*Use of Religion to Control Minds for Political Gain*	*52*
2.4.4	*Use of Science for the Development of Human Civilization*	*54*
Chapter III	**Psychological and Emotional Impacts**	**56-74**
3.1	*Psychological and Emotional Impacts: Science and Mental Health*	*56*

3.1.1	*The Benefits of a Scientific Mindset in Reducing Superstition and Anxiety*	*56*
3.1.2	*The Potential for Existential Crises in a Purely Materialistic Worldview*	*58*
3.2	*Religion and Mental Health:*	*62*
3.2.1	*The Comfort of Faith in Times of Uncertainty or Grief*	*62*
3.2.2	*The Risks of Dogmatic Thinking and Guilt Associated with Religious Beliefs*	*63*
3.2.3	*Manipulation and Violence in the Name of Religion*	*65*
3.2.4	*Balancing Faith and Mental Well-being*	*66*
3.3	*Case Studies*	*68*
3.3.1	*The Crossroads of Science and Faith: A Journey of the Mind and Soul*	*68*
3.3.2	*Individuals Who Have Embraced Science, Religion, or Both*	*68*
	Case Study 1: The Rationalist – Dr. Richard Dawkins	*69*
	Case Study 2: The Faithful Believer – Thomas Merton	*69*
	Case Study 3: The Bridging Mind – Dr. Francis Collins	*70*
3.4	*Psychological Profiles and Outcomes*	*71*
3.4.1	*The Rationalist's Psychological Landscape*	*71*
3.4.2	*The Devout Believer's Psychological Landscape*	*71*
3.4.3	*The Bridging Mind's Psychological Landscape*	*72*
3.4.4	*Embracing Diversity of Thought*	*72*
Chapter IV	**Education and Societal Influences**	**75-87**
4.1	*Science and Religion in Education*	*75*
4.1.1	*How Schools and Institutions Approach the Teaching of Science and Religion*	*75*
4.1.2	*The Impact of Education on Shaping Worldviews*	*77*
4.2	*Cultural and Societal Influences*	*80*
4.2.1	*Balancing Science and Religion: A Cultural Dilemma*	*81*
4.3	*The Role of Politics, Media and Technology in*	*82*

	Shaping Perceptions	
4.3.1	*Political Manipulation of Education*	*83*
4.3.2	*Media and the Spread of Misinformation*	*84*
4.3.3	*The Consequences of Neglecting Education*	*85*
Chapter V	**Bridging the Divide**	**89-101**
5.1	*Harmony Between Science and Religion:*	*89*
5.1.1	*Bridging the Divide: Harmony Between Science and Religion*	*89*
5.1.2	*Scientists Who Are Religious and Religious Figures Who Embrace Science*	*89*
5.1.3	*The Concept of "Non-Overlapping Magisteria*	*92*
5.1.4	*The Buddhist Perspective on Science*	*93*
5.2	*The Future of Science and Religion:*	*97*
5.2.1	*Emerging Trends in Spirituality and Scientific Discovery*	*97*
5.2.2	*How Mental Development Might Evolve in a World Increasingly Shaped by Technology and Globalization*	*98*
5.2.3	*Science as the Foundation of Human Civilization*	*99*
Chapter VI	**Conclusion**	**102-105**
6.1	*Summary of Key Insights:*	*102*
6.1.1	*The Complementary Roles of Science and Religion in Mental Development*	*102*
6.1.2	*The Importance of Fostering a Balanced Perspective*	*102*
6.2	*Final Thoughts*	*103*

PREFACE

The interplay between science and religion has been a subject of debate for centuries, shaping societies, cultures, and individual perspectives. While science is grounded in observation, experimentation, and evidence, religion is rooted in faith, tradition, and spirituality. *Science and Religion: The Battle for the Human Mind* delves into how these two powerful forces influence human thought, ethical values, and decision-making.

Through historical events and psychological studies, this book offers a balanced exploration of how science and religion contribute to mental development. Rather than asserting the superiority of one over the other, it encourages meaningful discussions on their coexistence and the potential for harmony between them.

My inspiration for writing this book comes from my father, the *late Lakhan Choudhary,* whose unwavering encouragement to question, analyze, and seek knowledge instilled in me a deep love for scientific inquiry from an early age. His influence, coupled with my academic background, sparked my curiosity about how belief systems shape human cognition and our perception of reality.

This book is built upon rigorous research, drawing from scholarly discussions and peer-reviewed sources to ensure credibility. I have endeavored to make the content engaging and accessible, inviting readers from all backgrounds to reflect on this thought-provoking subject.

I extend my heartfelt gratitude to my family, colleagues, and students whose insights have enriched my perspective. Special thanks to my readers, whose curiosity and enthusiasm have motivated me to present complex ideas in a simple yet profound manner.

I hope this book serves as a valuable resource for those interested in exploring the profound impact of science and religion on human thought. May it inspire deeper inquiry and open doors to meaningful conversations on this ever-relevant subject.

Dr. Shashi Bhushan
Asst. Professor,
Dept. of Botany
A.S. College, Bikramganj

Chapter I

Foundations of Science and Religion

1.1. Defining Science and Religion:

1.1.1. Science: The Spirit of Curiosity, Skepticism, and Evidence-Based Discovery

Imagine a time long before telescopes or satellites—when early humans looked up at the night sky, mesmerized by the tiny lights scattered across the darkness. What were they? Gods? Fires in the heavens? Rather than accepting myths or speculation, some curious minds chose to seek answers. They watched, measured, and recorded patterns in the stars, unknowingly laying the foundation for what we now call science.

At its core, science is driven by a relentless curiosity—a desire to understand the world not through guesswork, but through observation and evidence. This approach, known as empirical inquiry, has shaped our understanding of everything from the vastness of space to the microscopic world of cells. By questioning assumptions, testing ideas, and refining knowledge over time, science continues to uncover the mysteries of our universe.

Science isn't just about gathering data—it's about questioning everything. That's where skepticism comes in. Think of it as a mental filter, a way to separate fact from fiction. Scientists don't just accept ideas because they sound convincing or come from someone important. Instead, they ask, *"How do we know this is true? What evidence supports it?"*

Take Albert Einstein's theory of relativity, for example. When he first proposed it, it completely challenged Newton's long-accepted laws of physics. The scientific community didn't just take his word for it—they put his ideas to the test. Only after experiments confirmed his predictions, like the bending of light around the sun during a solar eclipse, did his theory gain acceptance. This constant process of questioning and testing is what makes scientific knowledge so reliable. At its heart, science is about uncovering truth through evidence. It's not based on personal beliefs or opinions but on facts that stand up to scrutiny. Consider Alexander Fleming's accidental discovery of penicillin. He wasn't looking for antibiotics—he was simply studying bacteria when he noticed something unusual: a mold called *Penicillium* was killing the bacteria in his petri dish. Instead of brushing it off as a fluke, he investigated further. His curiosity and persistence led to one of the greatest medical breakthroughs in history. This is the power of science—turning curiosity and chance into life-changing discoveries.

Science doesn't claim to have all the answers, and that's part of its strength. It's a journey, not a destination. Every discovery leads to new questions, and every answer is open to revision if new evidence emerges. For example, the theory of plate tectonics—the idea that Earth's crust is made up of moving plates—was once considered controversial. But as scientists gathered more data from earthquakes, volcanoes, and ocean floors, the theory became the foundation of modern geology. This willingness to adapt and grow is what makes science such a powerful tool for understanding the world.

In a way, science is like a detective story. It starts with a mystery—a question about how something works. Scientists gather clues through experiments and observations, piece together the evidence, and slowly uncover the truth. And just like in a good detective story, the journey is as exciting as the solution. Whether it's exploring the depths of the ocean, decoding the human genome, or searching for distant planets, science continues to push the boundaries of what we know, one piece of evidence at a time.

References

1. Sagan, C. (1980). *Cosmos*. Random House.
2. Bryson, B. (2003). *A Short History of Nearly Everything*. Broadway Books.
3. Isaacson, W. (2007). *Einstein: His Life and Universe*. Simon & Schuster.
4. Roach, M. (2010). *Packing for Mars: The Curious Science of Life in the Void*. W.W. Norton & Company.
5. Gould, S. J. (1999). *Rocks of Ages: Science and Religion in the Fullness of Life*. Ballantine Books.

1.1.2. Religion: Faith, spirituality, and the search for meaning beyond the material world.

Religion has long been heralded as a source of hope, guidance, and moral structure. However, beneath its seemingly benevolent facade lies a history tainted by division, exploitation, and violence. While faith and spirituality promise transcendence beyond the material world, they have also served as tools for control, manipulation, and destruction. The search for meaning, when confined to rigid religious doctrines, often leads to blind allegiance, intolerance, and an erosion of rational thought.

For centuries, religious institutions have wielded immense power, dictating societal norms and suppressing dissent. Wars have been fought in the name of religion, with countless lives lost in crusades, jihads, and inquisitions. Rather than uniting humanity, faith has often been the root of sectarian conflicts, from the blood-soaked battlefields of medieval Europe to the ongoing strife in the Middle East. Instead of fostering peace and understanding, religious differences have created barriers, leading to discrimination, oppression, and persecution of those who think differently.

Religious authorities have frequently manipulated the faithful, using divine justification to impose their own agendas. From the sale of indulgences in medieval Christianity to extremist ideologies in the modern world, religion has been used as a means of subjugation. Women, in particular, have suffered under religious dogma, with many faiths enforcing oppressive roles that limit their rights and freedoms. Rather than serving as a source of liberation, religion has too often been a chain that binds individuals to outdated traditions and injustices. The caste system in Hinduism, restrictions on female clergy in Christianity, and strict gender roles in Islam further exemplify the ways in which religion can hinder social progress.

Moreover, religion has been an impediment to scientific progress and critical thinking. Throughout history, scientific discoveries that contradicted religious teachings were met with fierce opposition. Galileo was condemned for his heliocentric model of the solar system, and Charles Darwin's theory of evolution remains a point of contention among religious fundamentalists. When belief is placed above reason, societies stagnate, clinging to myths and superstitions instead of embracing knowledge and progress. The influence of religious beliefs on public policies, such as opposition to stem cell research and climate change denial, continues to hinder advancements that could benefit humanity as a whole.

Even in modern times, religious extremism continues to pose a significant threat. Terrorist organizations justify atrocities through distorted interpretations of sacred texts, while radical preachers incite violence in the name of faith. Societal debates on issues such as LGBTQ+ rights, reproductive freedom, and secular governance remain mired in religious opposition, obstructing efforts to build a more inclusive and progressive world. Religious indoctrination, particularly in early childhood, prevents many individuals from developing independent, critical thinking skills, instead embedding in them a fear-based worldview that prioritizes faith over empirical evidence.

The intersection of politics and religion has further exacerbated these issues. Religious groups often wield disproportionate influence over governments, shaping laws that reflect religious morality rather than universal human rights. In nations where religious fundamentalism dominates, secular voices are silenced, and any deviation from prescribed beliefs is met with punishment. The enforcement of blasphemy laws, honor killings, and religious tribunals highlights how religious dogma can be wielded as a tool of oppression and control.

While faith may provide comfort to many, it has also been responsible for untold suffering. The search for meaning beyond the material world should not come at the cost of human rights, scientific advancement, or social cohesion. If religion is to have a place in the future, it must evolve beyond dogma, embrace rationality, and serve as a force for unity rather than division. The recognition of human dignity, freedom of thought, and the separation of church and state are necessary steps in ensuring that religion, if it persists, aligns with the ethical progress of society.

References:

1. Dawkins, R. (2006). *The God Delusion.* Houghton Mifflin Harcourt.
2. Hitchens, C. (2007). *God Is Not Great: How Religion Poisons Everything*. Twelve Books.
3. Harris, S. (2004). *The End of Faith: Religion, Terror, and the Future of Reason*. W.W. Norton & Company.
4. Dennett, D. (2006). *Breaking the Spell: Religion as a Natural Phenomenon*. Viking Press.
5. Armstrong, K. (2014). *Fields of Blood: Religion and the History of Violence*. Knopf.

1.1.3. Historical context of the science-religion debate.

The relationship between science and religion has evolved over centuries, shaped by cultural, philosophical, and intellectual developments. In many ancient civilizations, religious beliefs and scientific inquiry were not seen as conflicting but rather intertwined. Early scientific thought in Mesopotamia, Egypt, India, and China was often linked with religious and philosophical perspectives. However, with the rise of systematic rational inquiry in ancient Greece and India, questions about the natural world and the existence of divine beings became subjects of philosophical debate. One of the most striking historical instances of skepticism toward the concept of a creator deity can be found in Buddhism. Siddhartha Gautama, known as the Buddha, rejected the notion of an omnipotent creator god, arguing that the universe functions according to natural laws rather than divine intervention (Gombrich, 2009). His teachings emphasized empirical observation and personal experience over faith in a supernatural being, a perspective that in some ways aligns with the scientific method.

During the medieval period, religious institutions played a crucial role in preserving and disseminating scientific knowledge. Islamic scholars during the Golden

Age of Islam, such as Alhazen, made significant contributions to optics and mathematics while reconciling their findings with Islamic theology (Saliba, 2007). Similarly, in medieval Christian Europe, theologians like Thomas Aquinas sought to integrate Aristotelian philosophy with Christian doctrine. However, conflicts arose when scientific discoveries challenged religious orthodoxy. The most famous example is the trial of Galileo Galilei in the 17th century. His support for heliocentrism, based on the observational evidence gathered through his telescope, directly contradicted the geocentric model endorsed by the Catholic Church (Brooke, 1991). This event marked a turning point in the science-religion debate, symbolizing the struggle between emerging empirical evidence and established religious authority.

The 19th century brought further tensions, particularly with Charles Darwin's *On the Origin of Species* (1859), which proposed evolution by natural selection. This directly contradicted the creationist view held by many religious groups, leading to fierce debates that continue to this day (Numbers, 2009). However, despite these conflicts, many scholars and theologians have sought to reconcile scientific discoveries with religious belief. The idea that science and religion occupy "non-overlapping magisteria," as proposed by Stephen Jay Gould (1997), suggests that science addresses the empirical nature of the universe, while religion provides ethical and spiritual meaning.

In contemporary times, the debate has extended to issues such as bioethics, artificial intelligence, and the origins of the cosmos. While fundamentalist religious perspectives sometimes resist scientific explanations, many religious traditions have adapted, incorporating scientific insights into their worldviews. The historical trajectory of the science-religion debate suggests that while conflicts have occurred, science and religion have also coexisted and even complemented each other in shaping human understanding. From the Buddha's rejection of a creator deity to modern discussions on artificial intelligence and consciousness, the dialogue between science and religion continues to evolve, reflecting the complexity of human thought and inquiry.

References:

1. Brooke, J. H. (1991). *Science and Religion: Some Historical Perspectives.* Cambridge University Press.
2. Gombrich, R. (2009). *What the Buddha Thought.* Equinox Publishing.
3. Gould, S. J. (1997). *Nonoverlapping Magisteria.* Natural History.
4. Numbers, R. L. (2009). *Galileo Goes to Jail and Other Myths About Science and Religion.* Harvard University Press.
5. Saliba, G. (2007). *Islamic Science and the Making of the European Renaissance.* MIT Press.

1.2. Historical Perspectives:

1.2.1. Ancient Civilizations: Science and Religion as Intertwined

Science and religion were deeply interwoven in the ancient world, serving as two complementary means through which civilizations sought to understand the cosmos, human existence, and natural phenomena. In societies such as Mesopotamia, Egypt, India, China, and Greece, scientific endeavors were often pursued within a religious framework, with priests, scholars, and philosophers using religious principles to guide their observations and experiments. Rather than viewing science and religion as separate or opposing forces, these civilizations saw them as mutually reinforcing, where religious beliefs provided structure to scientific pursuits, and scientific discoveries deepened spiritual understanding.

1.2.2. Mesopotamia: Astronomy, Mathematics, and Divine Will

Mesopotamian civilization, one of the earliest cradles of human knowledge, saw science and religion as inseparable. Priests, who were also scholars, meticulously studied the movements of celestial bodies, believing that planetary motions were divine messages from the gods.

The Babylonians developed an advanced mathematical system based on a sexagesimal (base-60) numeral system, which was used for astronomical calculations and to predict celestial events such as eclipses (Rochberg, 2004). These astronomical records, inscribed on clay tablets, were essential not only for agricultural planning but also for religious ceremonies, as Mesopotamians believed that the positions of the stars and planets influenced the fate of their cities and rulers. The practice of divination, including hepatoscopy (examining the liver of sacrificial animals) and astrology, was based on the assumption that the divine communicated with humans through natural patterns (Oppenheim, 1977).

1.2.3. Egypt: Engineering, Medicine, and Spiritual Significance

In ancient Egypt, scientific advancements in engineering, medicine, and astronomy were closely tied to religious beliefs. The construction of the pyramids, which required a deep understanding of mathematics, geometry, and engineering, was motivated by religious doctrines concerning the afterlife. Egyptian mortuary practices, including mummification, demonstrated an advanced knowledge of human anatomy and chemistry, driven by the belief that preserving the body ensured the soul's journey into the afterlife (David, 2002). Egyptian medicine, largely practiced by temple priests, combined empirical observations with religious rituals. Medical texts such as the Edwin Smith Papyrus and the Ebers Papyrus reveal a sophisticated understanding of human physiology, disease diagnosis, and surgical techniques, while simultaneously attributing certain illnesses to supernatural causes and prescribing prayers and charms as treatments (Nunn, 1996).

1.2.4. India: Buddhism, Ayurveda, and Scientific Inquiry

Buddhism, which emerged in India in the 5th–6th century BCE, introduced a unique perspective on science and knowledge. Unlike many religious traditions that emphasized divine intervention, Buddhism placed significant emphasis on empirical observation, reason, and direct experience as means to understand the world. The Buddhist epistemological tradition, particularly in texts such as the *Abhidharma* and the works of Nagarjuna, explored the nature of reality, perception, and causality in a manner resembling scientific inquiry (Gethin, 1998).

Buddhist medicine, influenced by Ayurveda, developed systematic approaches to healing based on the balance of bodily humors and mindfulness practices. The spread of Buddhism across Asia facilitated the transmission of medical knowledge, including surgical techniques and herbal medicine, to regions such as China and Tibet. Additionally, Buddhist monastic institutions often served as centers for learning and research, where scholars engaged in astronomy, mathematics, and psychology while maintaining a spiritual foundation in their pursuits (Zysk, 1991).

1.2.5. China: Daoism, Confucianism, and the Natural World

In ancient China, science and religion were unified through Daoist and Confucian philosophies, which emphasized harmony between humans and nature. Chinese medicine, alchemy, and astronomy were deeply influenced by Daoist principles of balance (yin and yang) and the Five Elements (wood, fire, earth, metal, and water) (Needham, 1954). Traditional Chinese medicine (TCM), which included acupuncture, herbal remedies, and qigong (breath control exercises), was guided by the belief that health depended on the balance of qi (vital energy) within the body. This concept, though spiritual in nature, led to systematic medical practices that were refined over centuries.

Chinese astronomy, which played a crucial role in imperial governance and agriculture, was developed by court astronomers who meticulously recorded celestial events. These records were used to align the emperor's rule with cosmic order, as the "Mandate of Heaven" doctrine dictated that celestial disturbances could signify divine displeasure with the ruling dynasty. Alchemy in China, often associated with the search for immortality, contributed to the development of early chemistry and metallurgy, with Daoist alchemists experimenting with minerals and compounds that would later influence traditional medicine and gunpowder production (Ho, 1966).

1.2.6. Greece: Philosophical Rationalism and Mysticism

Ancient Greece is often credited with laying the foundations of Western scientific thought, yet its scholars operated within a deeply religious framework. Early Greek philosophers such as Thales, Anaximander, and Heraclitus sought to explain the natural world through rational principles rather than mythological narratives, yet their theories often retained mystical elements. Pythagoras, for instance, linked mathematics with religious mysticism, believing that numbers held divine significance and that geometric patterns reflected the fundamental order of the cosmos (Kirk et al., 1983).

Plato's philosophy blended metaphysical and scientific ideas, suggesting that the material world was a reflection of an ideal, divine realm. Aristotle, despite his empirical approach to biology, physics, and logic, also proposed a teleological view of nature, arguing that all things had an inherent purpose dictated by a "prime mover," a divine force responsible for the motion of the universe (Lindberg, 2007). Greek medicine, as practiced by Hippocrates and Galen, sought to understand diseases through natural causes, yet it remained influenced by religious ideas, including the belief that divine forces played a role in healing (Nutton, 2004).

Across ancient civilizations, science and religion were not seen as distinct or contradictory domains but rather as interconnected aspects of human understanding. Religious beliefs often provided motivation, structure, and ethical guidelines for scientific exploration, while empirical discoveries helped refine theological and philosophical concepts. The Buddhist perspective, in particular, introduced an epistemological approach that emphasized empirical experience and rational analysis, contributing to the broader intellectual landscape. This fusion of science and spirituality shaped intellectual traditions that influenced later scientific developments in medieval and modern times. By recognizing the historical interconnection between science and religion, we gain insight into how human civilizations have long sought to comprehend the mysteries of existence through both rational inquiry and spiritual contemplation.

References

1. David, R. (2002). *Religion and Magic in Ancient Egypt*. Penguin Books.
2. Gethin, R. (1998). *The Foundations of Buddhism*. Oxford University Press.
3. Ho, P. (1966). *The Laboratory Alchemist in Ancient China*. Harvard University Press.
4. Kirk, G. S., Raven, J. E., & Schofield, M. (1983). *The Presocratic Philosophers*. Cambridge University Press.
5. Lindberg, D. C. (2007). *The Beginnings of Western Science*. University of Chicago Press.
6. Needham, J. (1954). *Science and Civilization in China*. Cambridge University Press.

7. Nunn, J. F. (1996). *Ancient Egyptian Medicine*. British Museum Press.
8. Nutton, V. (2004). *Ancient Medicine*. Routledge.
9. Oppenheim, A. L. (1977). *Ancient Mesopotamia: Portrait of a Dead Civilization*. University of Chicago Press.
10. Rochberg, F. (2004). *The Heavenly Writing: Divination, Horoscopy, and Astronomy in Mesopotamian Culture*. Cambridge University Press.
11. Zysk, K. G. (1991). *Asceticism and Healing in Ancient India: Medicine in the Buddhist Monastery*. Oxford University Press.

1.3. The Enlightenment: The Rise of Scientific Reasoning and Its Challenge to Religious Dogma

It was a crisp autumn afternoon in the 1600s when a young Isaac Newton sat under an apple tree, deep in thought. As he watched an apple fall to the ground, a question arose in his mind: *Why did it fall straight down?* Was it merely the will of God, or was there an unseen force at work? Newton's search for answers would lead him to discover gravity, a force that governed the movement of everything from apples to planets. His discovery symbolized a great shift happening across Europe—the Enlightenment, a period when people began to seek knowledge through reason, observation, and experimentation rather than relying solely on religious explanations.

For centuries, religious authorities had shaped how people understood the world. The Church taught that the Earth was the center of the universe, with the sun, stars, and planets revolving around it, as ordained by divine design. But when scientists like Nicolaus Copernicus and Galileo Galilei looked through telescopes, they saw something different. The sun, not the Earth, was at the center of the solar system. Galileo's observations contradicted religious teachings, and when he openly supported the idea, the Church put him on trial. Forced to recant his findings,

Galileo spent the rest of his life under house arrest. However, his ideas had already taken root, inspiring others to question long-held beliefs.

Across Europe, philosophers like René Descartes and Francis Bacon encouraged people to seek truth through questioning and experimentation. Descartes famously declared, *"I think, therefore I am,"* suggesting that human reason, not faith, should be the foundation of knowledge. Bacon promoted the scientific method, insisting that knowledge should come from systematic observation and evidence. These ideas spread like wildfire in the coffeehouses and salons of London and Paris, where intellectuals debated the nature of government, human rights, and the role of religion in society.

One of the most outspoken critics of religious dogma was Voltaire, a French writer who challenged the Church's influence over knowledge and society. "If God did not exist," he wrote, "it would be necessary to invent him." To Voltaire and his fellow Enlightenment thinkers, religion was no longer an unquestionable authority but a human institution that should be scrutinized like any other. Meanwhile, political philosophers like John Locke and Jean-Jacques Rousseau questioned the divine right of kings, arguing that governments should be based on the will of the people, not on religious authority. These revolutionary ideas influenced the American and French Revolutions, leading to the rise of democracy and individual freedoms.

Even as science gained ground, many Enlightenment thinkers still believed in God. However, they saw the universe as a machine governed by natural laws rather than divine intervention. Newton himself believed that understanding the laws of nature was a way to appreciate God's design, but he insisted that science, not religious doctrine, should explain the workings of the world.

1.3.1. The Monk Who Brought Order to Nature

A century after Newton, another great thinker worked in quiet solitude, unaware that his discoveries would shake the foundations of biology. In a small monastery garden in Austria, Gregor Mendel, a humble monk, tended to his pea plants. Day after day, he carefully crossed different varieties, counting the colors, shapes, and sizes of the offspring. Unlike other gardeners, Mendel was not content with simply observing nature—he wanted to understand the hidden rules that governed inheritance.

At the time, most people believed that traits were blended together from both parents, much like mixing paint colors. But as Mendel meticulously recorded the traits of thousands of pea plants, he noticed patterns that no one else had seen. When he crossed tall and short plants, their offspring were not all medium-sized as expected. Instead, some were tall, some were short, and some seemed to carry hidden traits that reappeared in later generations.

Through years of painstaking experiments, Mendel uncovered the fundamental principles of inheritance. He discovered that traits were passed down through invisible "factors"—what we now call genes—and that they followed mathematical patterns. His findings, published in 1866, challenged traditional beliefs about biology, much like Newton's laws had challenged old ideas about physics.

However, Mendel's work went unnoticed during his lifetime. The scientific community, still under the influence of older theories, ignored his findings. It was only decades later, in the early 1900s, that biologists rediscovered his research and realized he had uncovered the basic rules of genetics. Today, Mendel is celebrated as the father of modern genetics, but in his own time, he remained an unknown monk, quietly recording his data in the monastery garden.

1.3.2. A Legacy of Reason and Discovery

By the end of the Enlightenment, the world had changed forever. The triumph of science over religious dogma paved the way for the Industrial Revolution, the advancement of medicine, and the expansion of democracy. The scientific method became the foundation of modern knowledge, shaping everything from physics to biology. The work of thinkers like Newton, Galileo, and Mendel proved that the universe was not controlled by supernatural forces alone—it followed logical, predictable laws that could be understood through reason.

The apple that fell before Newton and the pea plants that grew in Mendel's garden were more than just ordinary objects. They were symbols of human curiosity, reminders that progress comes not from blind faith, but from questioning, exploring, and seeking the truth. The torch of reason, lit during the Enlightenment, continues to burn brightly, guiding us toward new discoveries and a deeper understanding of the world.

References

1. Copernicus, N. (1543). *De revolutionibus orbium coelestium* (On the Revolutions of the Heavenly Spheres).

2. Galileo, G. (1632). *Dialogue Concerning the Two Chief World Systems*. Florence: G. B. Landini.
3. Newton, I. (1687). *Philosophiæ Naturalis Principia Mathematica*. London: Royal Society.
4. Descartes, R. (1637). *Discourse on the Method.*
5. Bacon, F. (1620). *Novum Organum.*
6. Voltaire. (1764). *Dictionnaire philosophique* (Philosophical Dictionary).
7. Locke, J. (1689). *Two Treatises of Government.*
8. Mendel, G. (1866). *Experiments on Plant Hybridization.* Proceedings of the Natural History Society of Brünn.
9. Darwin, C. (1859). *On the Origin of Species.* London: John Murray.

1.4. Modern Era: The Ongoing Tension and Dialogue Between Science and Religion

1.4.1. A Trial That Shook the World

On a humid July morning in 1925, the small town of Dayton, Tennessee, found itself at the center of a national storm. A high school teacher named John Scopes was put on trial for teaching evolution in his classroom, violating a state law that mandated the teaching of divine creation. The trial, later called the *Scopes Monkey Trial*, was more than just a legal case—it was a dramatic clash between faith and reason, between tradition and progress.

The courtroom was packed with spectators, some holding their Bibles tightly, others wearing skeptical expressions. On one side stood William Jennings Bryan, a deeply religious statesman who argued that teaching evolution would undermine morality and weaken society's faith in God. On the other side, Clarence Darrow, a passionate defender of scientific thought, asked a crucial question: "Must we deny facts simply because they do not align with ancient beliefs?"

Though Scopes was found guilty and fined, the trial marked a turning point. It forced people to confront a growing reality—the world was changing, and science was challenging long-held religious doctrines.

1.4.2. The Expanding Universe and the Mind of God

Despite the friction between science and religion, some figures found harmony between the two. One of them was Georges Lemaître, a Catholic priest and physicist who, in 1927, proposed a groundbreaking theory—that the universe was not static but expanding. This radical idea suggested that the cosmos had a beginning, which contradicted earlier scientific views of an eternal, unchanging universe. At first, even Einstein dismissed Lemaître's idea, calling it "abominable."

But soon, observational evidence began to support Lemaître's theory. Astronomer Edwin Hubble discovered that galaxies were moving away from each other, confirming that the universe was indeed expanding. Eventually, Lemaître's idea became what we now call the Big Bang Theory.

Ironically, while many religious leaders had resisted Darwin's theory of evolution, some found comfort in the idea of a cosmic beginning. Could this be the moment of creation described in religious texts? The Vatican itself eventually embraced the Big Bang theory, seeing it as compatible with faith. For Lemaître, science and religion were not enemies but two ways of understanding the same truth.

1.4.3. Mendel's Pea Plants: A Monk's Contribution to Science

Long before Darwin's theory of evolution ignited debates, another religious figure had quietly laid the foundation for modern genetics. In the mid-19th century, Gregor Mendel, an Augustinian monk, spent years meticulously breeding pea plants in the garden of his monastery. Through his experiments, he discovered that traits were inherited according to specific patterns—what we now call the laws of inheritance.

Mendel's work, however, was largely ignored during his lifetime. It was only decades later that scientists rediscovered his findings and realized their significance. His work provided the genetic basis for evolution, showing how traits pass from one generation to the next. Today, Mendel is celebrated as the father of genetics, proving that faith and science can coexist in the same mind

.

1.4.4. The Medical Revolution: Miracles and Ethics

As the 20th century progressed, medical science made astonishing advancements. Diseases that were once considered divine punishments—like leprosy and the plague—were now understood in scientific terms. The discovery of antibiotics, vaccines, and advanced surgical techniques saved countless lives.

Yet, with every breakthrough came ethical and religious dilemmas. The ability to manipulate human genes, for instance, raised profound questions. In 1978, when the first test-tube baby, Louise Brown, was born through in-vitro fertilization (IVF), religious leaders debated whether it was ethical to create life in a laboratory. Some saw it as a gift of science, while others feared it was a violation of natural law. The tension between medicine and religion continues today. Stem cell research, cloning, and artificial intelligence in healthcare are pushing ethical boundaries, sparking debates about the role of science in shaping human destiny. Should science dictate the future of humanity, or should there be spiritual and moral limits?

1.4.5. Climate Change: A Call for Unity?

In recent years, science and religion have found themselves in conflict once again—this time over climate change. While scientists overwhelmingly agree that human activities are driving global warming, some religious groups reject the evidence, arguing that climate change is either exaggerated or part of God's natural plan.

However, not all religious voices dismiss science. Pope Francis, in his 2015 encyclical *Laudato Si'*, called on the world to take urgent action to protect the environment. He emphasized that caring for the Earth is a moral responsibility, aligning religious ethics with scientific warnings. Similarly, many Buddhist leaders stress the importance of living in harmony with nature, seeing environmental destruction as a violation of spiritual balance.

Despite these efforts, resistance remains. Some political and religious groups continue to challenge climate policies, fearing they may disrupt economic growth or individual freedoms. The struggle between scientific facts and ideological beliefs is ongoing.

1.4.6. Artificial Intelligence and the Future of Faith

As the world moves into the era of artificial intelligence (AI), new questions emerge. Can machines possess consciousness? If AI becomes highly intelligent, what role will human intuition, morality, and faith play? Religious scholars and scientists alike are grappling with these questions. Some see AI as an opportunity—an advanced tool to improve healthcare, education, and daily life. Others fear it could challenge the very essence of what it means to be human. Could AI ever replace the need for religion, offering logical answers to life's deepest mysteries? Or will it force people to seek spiritual meaning more than ever before?

1.4.7. A Dialogue That Never Ends

Despite centuries of conflict, science and religion remain intertwined. Science provides knowledge and technological progress, while religion offers ethical guidance, purpose, and a sense of belonging. The tension between them is not a war to be won but a dialogue that continues to shape the human experience.

History shows that breakthroughs often spark resistance, but eventually, society finds ways to integrate new knowledge with existing beliefs. Just as Galileo's discoveries were once condemned but later accepted, and just as Mendel's work was overlooked but later celebrated, the conflicts of today may become the understanding of tomorrow.

As we move forward, the challenge remains: Can science and religion find common ground? Can they work together to answer the deepest questions of existence? Or will the tension between them continue, shaping the world in ways we have yet to imagine?

The conversation is far from over.

References

1. Larson, E. J. (1997). *Summer for the Gods: The Scopes Trial and America's Continuing Debate Over Science and Religion.* Basic Books.
2. Darwin, C. (1859). *On the Origin of Species.* London: John Murray.
3. Hawking, S. (1988). *A Brief History of Time.* Bantam Books.
4. Haught, J. F. (1995). *Science and Religion: From Conflict to Conversation.* Paulist Press.
5. Dalai Lama. (2005). *The Universe in a Single Atom: The Convergence of Science and Spirituality.* Broadway Books.
6. Pope Francis. (2015). *Laudato Si': On Care for Our Common Home.* Vatican Press.

7. Numbers, R. (2009). *Galileo Goes to Jail and Other Myths About Science and Religion*. Harvard University Press.
8. Oreskes, N., & Conway, E. M. (2010). *Merchants of Doubt: How a Handful of Scientists Obscured the Truth on Issues from Tobacco Smoke to Global Warming*. Bloomsbury Press.
9. Mukherjee, S. (2016). *The Gene: An Intimate History*. Scribner.

Chapter II

Cognitive Development and Worldview Formation

2.1. The Role of Science in Mental growth

Science has always been more than a collection of facts and theories—it is a way of thinking, questioning, and understanding the world. From childhood to adulthood, science plays a crucial role in shaping our cognitive abilities, influencing how we perceive problems, seek solutions, and make informed decisions. The earliest humans, faced with survival challenges, developed problem-solving skills that laid the foundation for scientific thinking. The discovery of fire was not just an accidental event but a turning point that required observation, experimentation, and refinement. Similarly, the invention of the wheel demonstrated early engineering skills, problem-solving, and innovative thinking. These advancements shaped human civilization and exemplify how science has always been integral to mental growth.

Imagine an early human who observed that rubbing two stones together produced sparks, leading to fire. This discovery was not immediate; it required repeated attempts, careful observation, and an understanding of cause and effect. Similarly, the wheel was not invented in a day—it resulted from years of trial and error, demonstrating an application of engineering principles before formal science even existed. These early innovations highlight how problem-solving and analytical thinking have been essential for survival and progress. This analysis explores the impact of science on mental growth, focusing on critical thinking, curiosity, skepticism, and decision-making.

2.1.1. Critical Thinking and Problem-Solving Skills

One of the most profound contributions of science to mental growth is its role in fostering critical thinking and problem-solving skills. Scientific inquiry teaches individuals to analyze data, recognize patterns, and evaluate evidence before drawing conclusions. Consider the case of Thomas Edison, who experimented with thousands of different materials before discovering the ideal filament for the electric bulb. His approach—testing hypotheses, learning from failures, and refining methods—is a perfect example of scientific problem-solving in action. From an early age, children exposed to science learn to approach problems systematically. When a child constructs a volcano using baking soda and vinegar, they unknowingly practice hypothesis testing—anticipating reactions, observing results, and modifying their approach based on outcomes. Such experiences build essential cognitive skills that extend beyond the classroom into everyday life, helping individuals navigate challenges with logic and resilience (Dunbar, 1995).

Additionally, scientific problem-solving is not limited to laboratories. Professionals in various fields, from engineers designing safer bridges to doctors diagnosing complex diseases, rely on scientific principles to solve real-world problems. A surgeon, for instance, follows evidence-based procedures to determine the best course of treatment, much like a scientist conducting experiments to confirm a hypothesis. This ability to apply logical reasoning to diverse situations is a testament to the transformative power of science on mental growth.

2.1.2. Encouraging Curiosity and Skepticism

Science does not merely provide answers; it fuels curiosity by encouraging people to ask questions. The history of scientific breakthroughs is filled with individuals who refused to accept conventional wisdom at face value. Galileo Galilei's observations of celestial bodies challenged the geocentric model of the universe, paving the way for modern astronomy. His willingness to question established beliefs exemplifies the essence of scientific skepticism. Today, this spirit of inquiry is embedded in educational systems through scientific experiments and explorations. For instance, when students engage in projects like testing water quality in their surroundings, they not only learn about pollution but also develop a habit of questioning and verifying information before accepting it as truth. This mindset extends into adulthood, empowering individuals to differentiate between misinformation and reliable knowledge, particularly in the digital age (Sagan, 1996).

Moreover, curiosity drives innovation. Great scientists such as Albert Einstein, who questioned the nature of time and space, and Marie Curie, who tirelessly researched radioactivity despite societal barriers, have reshaped our world. Their insatiable curiosity and skepticism towards accepted norms led to groundbreaking discoveries. Encouraging these traits in students and professionals alike ensures a future where progress is driven by inquiry rather than blind acceptance.

2.1.3. The Impact of Scientific Literacy on Decision-Making and Worldview

Scientific literacy goes beyond academic knowledge; it significantly shapes decision-making and worldview. A scientifically literate person can assess health information critically, distinguish between fact and fiction, and make informed choices. During the COVID-19 pandemic, individuals with a basic understanding of virology, epidemiology, and statistical reasoning were better equipped to interpret public health recommendations and make rational decisions about vaccinations and preventive measures (Lederman, 2013).

Moreover, science influences broader perspectives on global issues such as climate change, energy consumption, and medical advancements. Consider the case of renewable energy adoption. Communities that understand the science behind solar and wind energy are more likely to support sustainable policies and innovations. This demonstrates how scientific education fosters a worldview that values evidence-based reasoning and long-term planning.

Beyond public policy, scientific literacy also enhances personal choices. An individual aware of the nutritional value of different foods is more likely to adopt a healthy diet, reducing the risk of lifestyle diseases. Similarly, an awareness of genetic predispositions can lead to proactive health management. These examples highlight how science not only expands knowledge but also improves quality of life.

The role of science in mental growth is indispensable. By promoting critical thinking, nurturing curiosity and skepticism, and enhancing decision-making abilities, science equips individuals with cognitive tools that extend beyond laboratories and textbooks. As we navigate an increasingly complex world, fostering a scientific mindset will continue to be essential for individual growth and societal progress. A future driven by scientific thinking will lead to more innovative solutions, better decision-making, and a society that values evidence over superstition. Thus, integrating science deeply into education and everyday life is not just beneficial—it is necessary for sustainable development and progress.

References

3. Dunbar, K. (1995). How scientists really reason: Scientific reasoning in real-world laboratories. *Cognitive Psychology*, 27(3), 303-340.
4. Lederman, N. G. (2013). Nature of science: Past, present, and future. *Science & Education*, 22(3), 417-431.
5. Sagan, C. (1996). *The Demon-Haunted World: Science as a Candle in the Dark*. Ballantine Books.
6. Kuhn, T. S. (1962). *The Structure of Scientific Revolutions*. University of Chicago Press.
7. Popper, K. (1959). *The Logic of Scientific Discovery*. Routledge.

2.2. The Role of Religion in Mental growth

Religion has played a crucial role in shaping human civilization, influencing cultures, moral values, and mental growth. However, its impact on intellectual progress has often been negative, restricting independent thought and reinforcing dogmatic beliefs. By emphasizing faith over reason, religion discourages skepticism and inquiry, preventing individuals from questioning established doctrines. Many religious institutions have historically opposed scientific discoveries and philosophical advancements, branding them as heretical. This suppression of knowledge has stifled progress, leading to persecution of free thinkers such as Socrates, Galileo, and Bruno. Instead of fostering curiosity and exploration, religious traditions often demand blind adherence to sacred texts and the authority of religious leaders, discouraging critical thinking. In societies where religion dominates education and governance, individuals are conditioned to accept preordained truths rather than challenge them. Consequently, the mental growth of religious adherents is shaped by conformity rather than intellectual freedom, restricting their ability to engage in rational discourse and independent decision-making. Throughout history, religious doctrines have provided both stability and resistance to change, creating a complex relationship between faith, knowledge, and mental growth.

2.2.1. Conformity and Resistance to New Ideas

In a small village nestled between rolling hills, a young boy named Aarav was raised in a deeply religious household. Every morning, he would accompany his grandmother to the temple, listening to stories of gods and goddesses, morality, and the importance of faith. These stories shaped his worldview, giving him a sense of identity and purpose. However, as he grew older, he encountered new ideas in school—science, philosophy, and perspectives that questioned the beliefs he had held so dearly.

Aarav's initial reaction was resistance. The familiar comfort of his religious teachings clashed with the novelty of scientific explanations. He saw this struggle in his peers as well—some adhered strictly to the beliefs instilled in them, while others embraced change with enthusiasm. Religion, in many ways, had nurtured his intellectual foundation, but it also imposed limits on his willingness to explore beyond its borders. The community around him valued conformity, and breaking away from traditional thought was often seen as a rebellion rather than growth. Religious individuals often do not engage in critical thinking and refuse to accept new ideas, following the same path directed by religious leaders or sacred texts. This pattern can be observed throughout history, such as the execution of Socrates, the persecution of Galileo, and the Church's resistance to Darwin's theory of evolution.

2.2.2. Luck, and Resistance to Change

As Aarav matured, he observed another intriguing aspect of religion—its relationship with luck. His mother often credited divine intervention for success and blamed misfortunes on a lack of devotion. When Aarav studied probability and randomness in school, he began to see events through a different lens. Were the village's droughts truly a test from the gods, or were they a result of changing weather patterns?

This newfound awareness created tension within him. Religion had provided a structured way to interpret life's uncertainties, but he now questioned whether blind faith in luck and destiny hindered his ability to take control of his future. Many villagers remained steadfast in their beliefs, resisting any notion that removed divine influence from their lives. Aarav wondered—did this resistance to change prevent progress, or did it offer emotional resilience in times of hardship?

Historically, religious institutions have shown a strong resistance to change. The Catholic Church, for example, opposed the heliocentric model proposed by Copernicus and Galileo. Similarly, Darwin's theory of evolution was met with fierce opposition from religious authorities who saw it as a direct challenge to biblical creation narratives. Such resistance often stems from a rigid adherence to tradition rather than openness to new ideas.

2.2.3. Challenges of Critical Thinking

Aarav's journey reached a turning point when he left his village for university. Here, critical thinking was not just encouraged but required. He found himself surrounded by people who debated religious beliefs with logic and reason. Some viewed faith as an obstacle to intellectual growth, while others believed it provided ethical guidance and emotional support.

One evening, during a heated discussion with his professor, Aarav realized the true challenge of critical thinking—balancing faith and reason. Religion had given him a moral compass, a community, and a sense of purpose. But it had also, at times, discouraged questioning and exploration. He saw the same struggle in others: the challenge of holding onto beliefs while remaining open to inquiry.

From a psychological perspective, religious individuals often believe that divine intervention will resolve their problems rather than taking active steps to address them. This passive approach can hinder personal development and problem-solving abilities. Studies in psychology have shown that an external locus of control—where individuals believe external forces dictate their lives—can reduce motivation to find practical solutions.

As Aarav navigated this inner conflict, he understood that religion's role in mental growth was both profound and complex. It could nurture discipline and resilience, yet it could also create barriers to intellectual growth. The key, he realized, was not in outright rejection or blind acceptance, but in the ability to think critically while respecting the foundations that shaped him. And so, Aarav's journey continued—not as a skeptic or a devout follower, but as a seeker, forever questioning, learning, and evolving.

References

8. Dawkins, R. (2006). *The God Delusion.* Bantam Books.
9. Dennett, D. (2006). *Breaking the Spell: Religion as a Natural Phenomenon.* Viking.
10. Gould, S. J. (1997). *Rock of Ages: Science and Religion in the Fullness of Life*. Ballantine Books.
11. Harris, S. (2004). *The End of Faith: Religion, Terror, and the Future of Reason.* W.W. Norton & Company.
12. Wilson, E. O. (1998). *Consilience: The Unity of Knowledge*. Vintage Books.

2.3. Comparative Analysis between Science and Religion

Science and religion, two fundamental aspects of human civilization, have played pivotal roles in shaping societies, cultures, and individuals. While science relies on empirical reasoning, evidence-based conclusions, and experimental verification, religion is rooted in faith, spirituality, and moral guidance. The interplay between these two domains has led to both conflicts and harmonies throughout history. Understanding their roles in human cognition, their conflicts, and their contributions to civilization can offer deeper insights into their significance in contemporary society. This comparative analysis will delve into the ways science and religion influence human thought, their conflicts and synergies, and their impact on governance and societal progress. Science and religion influence human thought in fundamentally different ways, shaping how individuals perceive and interpret the world around them.

2.3.1. Science and Rational Thinking

Science fosters a mindset that values skepticism, inquiry, and systematic observation. It encourages individuals to question existing beliefs, experiment with new ideas, and rely on objective evidence to draw conclusions. This approach has led to remarkable discoveries that challenge conventional wisdom. For instance, the discovery of the heliocentric model by Copernicus contradicted the long-standing religious view that the Earth was the center of the universe. Similarly, modern medical advancements have debunked age-old superstitions about diseases being divine punishments.

The scientific method emphasizes logical reasoning and peer-reviewed validation, reducing reliance on anecdotal evidence and subjective interpretations. It has also led to innovations in technology, medicine, and engineering that have significantly improved human life. Education systems based on scientific reasoning cultivate critical thinking skills that empower individuals to make informed decisions in various aspects of life.

2.3.2. Religion and Faith-Based Thinking

On the other hand, religion nurtures belief systems based on faith, tradition, and moral philosophy. It provides individuals with a sense of purpose, ethical direction, and an understanding of existence beyond the physical world. Religious doctrines often serve as a foundation for social order, teaching values such as compassion, honesty, and humility.

A prime example of this is the influence of Buddhism on mindfulness and meditation practices. Ancient religious traditions that emphasized inner peace and self-awareness are now being studied scientifically for their psychological benefits. Additionally, religious texts and teachings have historically shaped laws, ethics, and customs in various cultures, guiding personal and communal behavior.

2.4. The Potential Conflicts and Synergies Between Empirical Reasoning and Faith-Based Beliefs

2.4.1. Conflicts Between Science and Religion

The historical tension between science and religion often arises from their differing methodologies and conclusions. While science relies on verifiable evidence, religion often depends on scriptures and divine revelations that may not be empirically tested. One of the most notable conflicts occurred during the trial of Galileo Galilei, who supported the Copernican model and was persecuted by the Catholic Church for challenging religious dogma.

Another prominent conflict exists in the debate over evolution. Charles Darwin's theory of evolution by natural selection contradicted the biblical creation narrative, leading to resistance from religious groups. Even today, debates over teaching evolution in schools continue, with some advocating for creationist perspectives based on religious beliefs.

Scientific discoveries have also raised ethical and theological questions. For example, advancements in genetic engineering, artificial intelligence, and reproductive technologies challenge traditional religious views on life, identity, and human intervention in natural processes.

2.4.2. Synergies Between Science and Religion

Despite their conflicts, science and religion have also found common ground. Many scientific pioneers, such as Isaac Newton, were deeply religious and saw their scientific work as a means of understanding divine creation. Additionally, several religious organizations support scientific advancements in medicine, environmental conservation, and technology. The Dalai Lama, for instance, has encouraged dialogue between Buddhism and neuroscience to explore consciousness and human well-being.

Modern psychology has also found parallels between religious practices and scientific findings. For example, prayer and meditation, integral to many religious traditions, have been shown to reduce stress and improve mental health. The synergy between science and religion is evident in institutions like the Vatican Observatory, which supports astronomical research while adhering to religious principles.

2.4.3. Use of Religion to Control Minds for Political Gain

Religion has shaped societies for centuries, but it has also been used as a tool for political control. Throughout history, leaders have twisted religious beliefs to justify their rule, silence critics, and keep people in line. In Middle Ages, for example—kings claimed they ruled by "divine right," meaning they were chosen by God. This made it seem like challenging their power wasn't just rebellion but a sin, discouraging people from speaking out. Even today, religion is often used to gain power and divide people. Extremist groups, impose strict religious rules to control society, often targeting women's rights and education. In many countries, politicians manipulate religious feelings to influence elections and strengthen their grip on power. A common tactic is religious nationalism—where leaders emphasize religious identity to gain support while sidelining minority groups. This strategy is used to justify controversial policies, often creating deeper divisions in society.

Beyond politics, religion also affects personal morality in surprising ways. The idea that "if people believe they can erase their sins, they may not stop sinning" raises an interesting debate. If someone thinks they can easily be forgiven—through prayer, repentance, or rituals—they might feel less pressure to avoid wrongdoing in the first place. While religion is meant to encourage good behavior, some people use it as a way to excuse dishonesty or harmful actions. This raises an important question: Does religion truly make people more responsible, or does it sometimes give them an easy way to avoid consequences? The answer likely depends on how individuals interpret and practice their faith.

The connection between religion, politics, and morality is complex. Religion can provide guidance, hope, and purpose, but it can also be exploited for control and manipulation. Whether it becomes a force for good or a tool for power depends on how it is used—by leaders, institutions, and individuals alike.

2.4.4. Use of Science for the Development of Human Civilization

Unlike the use of religion for political control, science has been a driving force behind human progress. Scientific advancements have led to breakthroughs in medicine, agriculture, and technology, improving the quality of life worldwide. For instance, the development of vaccines has eradicated deadly diseases like smallpox, significantly increasing human life expectancy.

The Industrial Revolution, fueled by scientific discoveries, transformed economies and societies by enhancing productivity and technological innovation. More recently, space exploration has expanded humanity's understanding of the universe, with missions like the Mars Rover providing valuable insights into the potential for extraterrestrial life.

Furthermore, scientific research has played a critical role in addressing global challenges, such as climate change. Renewable energy sources, such as solar and wind power, have emerged as sustainable solutions to reduce dependence on fossil fuels. The application of science in fields like artificial intelligence and biotechnology continues to shape the future of civilization, offering solutions to complex problems that humanity faces today.

Science and religion have been influential in shaping human thought, culture, and civilization. While they often come into conflict due to their differing approaches to truth and knowledge, they also offer complementary insights into the human experience. Science drives innovation and progress, while religion provides moral and ethical guidance. Recognizing both their strengths and limitations allows for a balanced perspective, promoting dialogue and mutual respect between these two fundamental forces of human society.

References

1. Dawkins, R. (2006). *The God Delusion*. Bantam Books.
2. Kuhn, T. S. (1962). *The Structure of Scientific Revolutions*. University of Chicago Press.
3. Wilson, E. O. (1998). *Consilience: The Unity of Knowledge*. Vintage Books.
4. Dalai Lama. (2005). *The Universe in a Single Atom: The Convergence of Science and Spirituality*. Harmony Books.
5. Gould, S. J. (1997). *Nonoverlapping Magisteria*. Natural History Magazine.
6. Numbers, R. (2009). *Galileo Goes to Jail and Other Myths about Science and Religion*. Harvard University Press.

Chapter III

Psychological and Emotional Impacts

3.1. Psychological and Emotional Impacts: Science and Mental Health

3.1.1. The Benefits of a Scientific Mindset in Reducing Superstition and Anxiety

Ravi grew up in a small village where every mishap was attributed to supernatural forces. If someone fell ill, whispers of curses and evil eyes spread faster than any medical diagnosis. But his world changed when he moved to the city for higher education. He was introduced to the scientific method—the process of questioning, testing, and reasoning. Slowly, the ghosts of superstition that haunted his thoughts began to fade. He realized that diseases had microbial origins, not supernatural causes, and weather patterns followed scientific principles, not divine punishments.

A scientific mindset fosters critical thinking, which, in turn, reduces irrational fears. Studies have shown that people who rely on scientific reasoning experience lower levels of anxiety. For instance, research conducted by Lindeman and Aarnio (2007) found that individuals with a higher inclination toward scientific thinking were less prone to magical beliefs, which are often linked to heightened anxiety and stress. When individuals understand the world through empirical evidence rather than superstition, they feel a greater sense of control over their lives. This self-efficacy, as described by Bandura (1997), plays a crucial role in reducing stress and enhancing mental well-being.

Another compelling example is the public perception of vaccines. In communities where science education is strong, people are less likely to succumb to the fear of vaccines causing autism—a myth debunked by countless studies (Taylor et al., 2014). Instead, they understand that vaccines are a triumph of scientific advancement, protecting millions from deadly diseases. By replacing fear with knowledge, science has the power to alleviate unnecessary emotional distress and empower individuals to make rational decisions.

A striking illustration of the difference between critical thinking and superstition is the accidental discovery of the microwave oven. Percy Spencer, an engineer working with radar technology, noticed that a chocolate bar in his pocket had melted while he was near an active magnetron. Curious, he conducted further experiments and soon realized that microwaves could be harnessed for cooking food. His scientific approach led to a revolutionary household appliance. However, imagine if a deeply religious person, lacking critical thinking skills, had observed the same phenomenon. Instead of investigating the cause, they might have attributed the melting chocolate to divine intervention or some supernatural force, missing out on a groundbreaking discovery. This stark contrast highlights how scientific inquiry drives progress, while a lack of it can perpetuate ignorance and misplaced beliefs.

3.1.2. The Potential for Existential Crises in a Purely Materialistic Worldview

However, the scientific approach to understanding reality is not without its psychological challenges. While science can debunk superstitions, it can also strip away comforting illusions, sometimes leading to existential anxiety. Ananya, a passionate astrophysicist, spent her life unraveling the mysteries of the cosmos. Yet, as she delved deeper into the vastness of space and the randomness of existence, she found herself grappling with a profound sense of insignificance. If humans are just a collection of atoms in a cold, indifferent universe, does life have any inherent meaning?

This kind of existential crisis is well-documented in psychology. Victor Frankl, in his book *Man's Search for Meaning* (1946), argues that humans need a sense of purpose to thrive. When individuals adopt a strictly materialistic view—where life is seen as nothing more than chemical reactions—it can lead to feelings of emptiness and despair. Studies in existential psychology, such as those by Yalom (1980), suggest that confronting the meaningless nature of existence can either lead to depression or, conversely, inspire people to create their own meaning through relationships, creativity, and personal growth.

A real-world example of this dilemma can be seen in the increasing popularity of existential therapy, which helps individuals cope with the anxiety of an indifferent universe by encouraging them to construct personal meaning. Scientific advancements in neuroscience have also shown that humans are wired to seek purpose, and lack of it is often linked to depression (Heisel & Flett, 2014). The challenge, therefore, is to balance scientific understanding with the innate human need for meaning and purpose.

Science, as a way of thinking, offers profound psychological benefits—it dispels irrational fears, promotes rational decision-making, and empowers individuals. However, it also comes with the emotional challenge of reconciling human existence with a universe that appears indifferent. The key lies in integrating scientific understanding with a philosophical approach that acknowledges the necessity of meaning. As Carl Sagan aptly said, “Science is not only compatible with spirituality; it is a profound source of spirituality.” While science may explain *how* we exist, the search for *why* remains a deeply personal journey.

References

6. Bandura, A. (1997). *Self-Efficacy: The Exercise of Control*. W.H. Freeman.
7. Frankl, V. (1946). *Man's Search for Meaning*. Beacon Press.
8. Heisel, M. J., & Flett, G. L. (2014). Purpose in life, satisfaction with life, and suicide ideation in older adults. *The Gerontologist, 54*(2), 259-268.
9. Lindeman, M., & Aarnio, K. (2007). Superstitious, magical, and paranormal beliefs: An integrative

model. *Journal of Research in Personality, 41*(4), 731-744.

10. Taylor, L. E., Swerdfeger, A. L., & Eslick, G. D. (2014). Vaccines are not associated with autism: An evidence-based meta-analysis of case-control and cohort studies. *Vaccine, 32*(29), 3623-3629.
11. Yalom, I. D. (1980). *Existential Psychotherapy*. Basic Books.

3.2. Religion and Mental Health:

3.2.1. The Comfort of Faith in Times of Uncertainty or Grief

The night was heavy with silence, except for the muffled cries of Maria as she sat by her mother's hospital bed. A devout woman, Maria had always turned to her faith in difficult times, but now, as her mother's health deteriorated, she felt an unbearable weight of helplessness. It was during one of these tearful nights that her local priest visited, holding her hands and praying with her. In that moment, Maria felt a deep sense of calm, as if the chaos in her mind had found an anchor.

This is not an isolated experience. Studies have long suggested that religion serves as a source of comfort in times of crisis. A study published in *The Journal of Religion and Health* (Koenig, 2012) found that individuals who actively engage in religious practices report lower levels of anxiety and depression, especially during periods of grief or uncertainty. Faith provides a sense of hope and continuity, which can be crucial in maintaining emotional stability.

A well-documented example is the aftermath of 9/11. Many survivors and victims' families turned to religious communities for support. Places of worship became sanctuaries where individuals could share their pain, find solace in scripture, and engage in collective mourning. Psychological research has shown that spirituality can help individuals reframe trauma, turning suffering into a journey of resilience and meaning-making (Pargament, 1997).

3.2.2. The Risks of Dogmatic Thinking and Guilt Associated with Religious Beliefs

While faith can offer comfort during times of suffering, it can also become a source of significant psychological distress when tied to rigid doctrines. Ravi, a bright college student, was raised in an environment where religious expectations were unyielding. He was taught that questioning faith was sinful, and any deviation from religious norms would result in punishment in the afterlife. When doubts began to surface, he felt overwhelmed by guilt and fear, as though he were betraying both his family and God. This emotional burden became so consuming that it triggered severe anxiety and depression.

Such struggles are not isolated. Dogmatic religious beliefs can lead to psychological conflicts, particularly when individuals are unable to reconcile their faith with personal doubts or modern scientific understanding. A study published in *Psychology of Religion and Spirituality* (Exline & Rose, 2005) underscores that religious guilt, particularly when linked to perceived moral failings, can contribute to anxiety, depression, and diminished self-esteem.

Historically, religious movements that promote extreme asceticism have also shown similar patterns. Followers are often led to believe that suffering and deprivation are essential for spiritual purity, leading them to experience chronic guilt, a diminished sense of self-worth, and an inability to seek help due to the fear of religious condemnation.

Karl Marx famously described religion as the "opium of the people," suggesting that it serves as a tool for numbing the pain of societal oppression. In this view, religion provides solace to the oppressed, but it also discourages individuals from challenging the structures that cause their suffering. This perspective reflects how certain interpretations of religion may, ironically, contribute to mental distress by fostering a sense of powerlessness and resignation, rather than encouraging personal liberation or change.

3.2.3. Manipulation and Violence in the Name of Religion

Religious devotion can sometimes make individuals susceptible to manipulation. Leaders or extremist groups may exploit faith for political or personal gain, leading followers to engage in harmful actions they might otherwise never consider. Throughout history, various religious movements have been used to justify violence, discrimination, and even mass killings.

One glaring example is the Crusades, a series of religious wars sanctioned by the Church, where thousands were killed in the name of Christianity. Similarly, extremist groups like ISIS have used religious rhetoric to justify acts of terrorism, claiming divine approval for their actions.

More recently, instances of religiously motivated violence have surfaced worldwide, including lynchings, honor killings, and terrorist attacks driven by ideological fanaticism. The 2002 Gujarat riots in India, where religious violence led to mass killings and displacement, showcase how religious sentiments can be manipulated to incite hatred and conflict. Psychological studies suggest that when individuals perceive their faith as being under threat, they may become more susceptible to radicalization and justifications for violence (Haidt, 2012).

3.2.4. Balancing Faith and Mental Well-being

Like any force in life, religion has the potential to be both a source of healing and a source of distress. The key lies in balance. Faith should empower individuals, offering them comfort and strength rather than fear and self-reproach. Religious communities that promote open discussions, compassion over dogma, and psychological well-being alongside spiritual practices tend to nurture healthier emotional lives for their members.

A hopeful shift is occurring in many religious circles today. More faith-based organizations are collaborating with mental health professionals to address the psychological needs of their congregations. Spiritual leaders are increasingly recognizing that mental health struggles are not signs of weak faith but part of the human condition, requiring empathy and professional intervention.

As Maria sat in her church, weeks after her mother's passing, she listened to a sermon about love and resilience. She realized that faith was not about fearing the unknown but about finding the courage to navigate it with hope. Meanwhile, Ravi found solace in a faith community that encouraged exploration and doubt as natural aspects of spiritual growth. Their stories, like so many others, highlight the profound and complex relationship between religion and mental health.

References

1. Koenig, H. G. (2012). Religion, spirituality, and health: The research and clinical implications. *International Scholarly Research Notices.*
2. Pargament, K. I. (1997). *The psychology of religion and coping: Theory, research, and practice.* Guilford Press.
3. Exline, J. J., & Rose, E. (2005). Religious and spiritual struggles: Implications for mental health and well-being. *Psychology of Religion and Spirituality.*
4. Haidt, J. (2012). *The Righteous Mind: Why Good People Are Divided by Politics and Religion.* Vintage.

3.3. Case Studies:

3.3.1. The Crossroads of Science and Faith: A Journey of the Mind and Soul

For centuries, humanity has sought answers to life's greatest mysteries through both scientific inquiry and religious faith. While some individuals find solace in one path, others embrace both, weaving together the realms of reason and spirituality. This interplay profoundly impacts psychological and emotional well-being. Through real-life case studies and research insights, we explore the psychological profiles and outcomes of those who have embraced science, religion, or both.

3.3.2. Individuals Who Have Embraced Science, Religion, or Both

Case Study 1: The Rationalist – Dr. Richard Dawkins

Dr. Richard Dawkins, an evolutionary biologist and prominent advocate for atheism, was raised in a religious household but later transitioned to a purely scientific worldview. His work in genetics and evolution, particularly through books like *The God Delusion*, emphasizes a rationalist approach to understanding existence. His psychological profile reveals high levels of analytical thinking, self-efficacy, and a structured cognitive framework. Dawkins' rational approach provides him with a sense of control over uncertainties. However, this also comes with existential anxiety, as he has openly discussed the challenges of finding meaning without a religious foundation. A study by Norenzayan and Gervais (2013) suggests that individuals who rely solely on scientific reasoning tend to experience higher degrees of existential dread but also exhibit greater resilience in handling uncertainty. In times of personal crisis, rationalists often turn to philosophical discourse or humanist principles rather than religious comfort.

Case Study 2: The Faithful Believer – Thomas Merton

Thomas Merton was a Trappist monk and renowned theologian who originally pursued a secular academic career before embracing a deeply religious life. In his early years, Merton explored literature and philosophy, but an existential crisis led him to Catholicism, eventually joining a monastery. His writings, such as *The Seven Storey Mountain*, detail his spiritual transformation and the profound peace he found in faith.

Religious faith provided Merton with emotional stability and a clear moral compass. Psychological assessments of devout believers, as explored by Koenig, King, and Carson

(2012), indicate that religious individuals often report better mental health outcomes due to social support systems and moral clarity. However, Merton also faced moments of doubt, which he resolved through deep theological contemplation. His ability to find meaning within faith demonstrates the psychological adaptability of religious individuals in integrating doubt without losing their belief.

Case Study 3: The Bridging Mind – Dr. Francis Collins

Dr. Francis Collins, a geneticist and former director of the National Institutes of Health (NIH), exemplifies the intersection of science and faith. Raised in a secular household, Collins converted to Christianity after encountering the writings of C.S. Lewis. Despite his deep commitment to scientific discovery—leading the Human Genome Project—he maintains a strong religious faith, advocating for the compatibility of science and belief through his book *The Language of God.*

Psychological analysis of Collins indicates high cognitive flexibility and emotional intelligence. He seamlessly navigates between scientific skepticism and faith-based introspection, allowing him to maintain a balanced psychological state. A study by Newberg, D'Aquili, and Rause (2001) highlights that individuals who embrace both science and religion tend to experience lower stress levels and a greater sense of purpose. Collins sees no conflict between evolutionary biology and belief in a divine creator, demonstrating that embracing both perspectives can enhance psychological well-being.

3.4. Psychological Profiles and Outcomes

3.4.1. The Rationalist's Psychological Landscape

The rationalist, like Dr. Dawkins, often exhibits high analytical thinking, strong problem-solving abilities, and cognitive resilience. These individuals approach life with a structured, evidence-based mindset, allowing them to navigate challenges with logic and reason. However, this approach comes with its drawbacks. Rationalists frequently experience existential anxiety as they struggle with questions of meaning and purpose beyond what can be empirically proven. They may also find it difficult to derive emotional comfort from abstract scientific principles, leading to occasional psychological distress.

3.4.2. The Devout Believer's Psychological Landscape

Faithful believers, like Thomas Merton, benefit from strong social support networks, emotional stability, and a clear moral framework. Religious faith often provides a strong sense of community, offering psychological reassurance in times of hardship. However, some challenges exist. Devout believers may exhibit cognitive rigidity, making it difficult for them to adapt to conflicting ideas. They may also struggle with fear of doubt, leading to distress when confronted with questions that challenge their beliefs. Nonetheless, their overall life satisfaction tends to be high due to the emotional and social security provided by their faith.

3.4.3. The Bridging Mind's Psychological Landscape

Individuals like Dr. Collins, who integrate both science and religion, exhibit cognitive flexibility, emotional balance, and an expanded capacity for wonder. These individuals can explore life's mysteries through both empirical evidence and spiritual insight, allowing them to navigate uncertainty with ease. However, they may occasionally experience ideological tension, toggling between faith and skepticism. Despite this, their ability to accept and embrace paradoxes often leads to greater psychological adaptability and overall well-being.

3.4.4. Embracing Diversity of Thought

The psychological and emotional impacts of embracing science, faith, or a combination of both vary significantly among individuals. Each path presents unique challenges and benefits, shaping cognitive frameworks, emotional resilience, and life satisfaction. Research suggests that individuals who successfully balance both perspectives tend to experience enhanced mental well-being. By acknowledging the psychological dimensions of belief and reason, we can cultivate a deeper understanding of human thought and behavior, fostering a more inclusive and open-minded society.

References

- Koenig, H. G., King, D. E., & Carson, V. B. (2012). *Handbook of Religion and Health*. Oxford University Press.
- Newberg, A., D'Aquili, E., & Rause, V. (2001). *Why God Won't Go Away: Brain Science and the Biology of Belief*. Ballantine Books.
- Norenzayan, A., & Gervais, W. M. (2013). *The Origins of Religious Disbelief: A Dual Process*

Model of Religious Cognition. Trends in Cognitive Sciences, 17(4), 186-192.

- Dawkins, R. (2006). *The God Delusion.* Bantam Press.
- Collins, F. (2006). *The Language of God: A Scientist Presents Evidence for Belief.* Free Press.
- Merton, T. (1948). *The Seven Storey Mountain.* Harcourt Brace.

Chapter IV

Education and Societal Influences

4.1. Science and Religion in Education

4.1.1. How Schools and Institutions Approach the Teaching of Science and Religion

Education is often considered the cornerstone of societal progress, shaping young minds and influencing worldviews. Schools and institutions serve as crucial platforms where scientific knowledge and religious beliefs intersect, sometimes harmoniously and at other times contentiously. Across the world, the approach to teaching science and religion varies significantly, influenced by cultural, political, and historical contexts.

In many secular education systems, such as those in the United States and most of Europe, science education follows a rigorous curriculum grounded in empirical evidence and the scientific method. Subjects like biology, physics, and chemistry are taught with an emphasis on observation, experimentation, and critical thinking. Religious studies, when included, are often presented as a separate discipline, aimed at fostering cultural understanding rather than endorsing particular beliefs.

However, debates continue about the inclusion of topics like evolution versus intelligent design in school curricula. In 2005, the Dover trial (Kitzmiller v. Dover Area School District) in the U.S. ruled that intelligent design could not be taught in public school science classes as it was considered a religious viewpoint rather than a scientific theory (Forrest & Gross, 2007).

Contrastingly, in many religiously affiliated institutions, the teaching of science is sometimes intertwined with faith-based perspectives. For instance, in Islamic schools (madrasas), Christian academies, and Hindu gurukuls, scientific concepts are often contextualized within theological frameworks. In some cases, scientific theories that conflict with religious teachings may be omitted or reinterpreted. Countries like Saudi Arabia and Iran integrate religious perspectives into their education systems, shaping how subjects such as human origins, cosmology, and medical ethics are taught (Eickelman, 1992).

4.1.2. The Impact of Education on Shaping Worldviews

The way science and religion are taught has a profound impact on how individuals perceive the world. Education plays a pivotal role in shaping worldviews, influencing opinions on critical issues such as climate change, medicine, and human rights. Societies with a strong emphasis on scientific literacy tend to exhibit higher acceptance of evidence-based. policies and technological advancements.

A striking example of education's influence can be observed in the global response to climate change. Nations with robust science education systems, such as Germany and Sweden, have been at the forefront of adopting sustainable practices and green technologies. A 2019 Pew Research Center study found that individuals with higher education levels are more likely to acknowledge climate change as a significant threat and support environmental policies (Pew Research Center, 2019).

Conversely, in societies where religious doctrine heavily influences education, perspectives on scientific issues can differ significantly. In some communities, vaccine hesitancy has been linked to religious beliefs, affecting public health. For example, in Nigeria, misinformation regarding the polio vaccine led to widespread resistance in the early 2000s, delaying eradication efforts (Jegede, 2007). Similarly, debates over the acceptance of evolutionary theory continue in parts of the United States where religious fundamentalism is prevalent, impacting students' understanding of biology and anthropology. Despite these differences, education also serves as a bridge between science and religion. Institutions like Harvard Divinity School and Oxford's Ian Ramsey Centre for Science and Religion work to create dialogues that reconcile faith with scientific reasoning. By fostering interdisciplinary approaches, such initiatives help students appreciate both the empirical rigor of science and the ethical, philosophical dimensions of religious beliefs.

Ultimately, education is not merely a transfer of knowledge; it is a powerful tool that shapes how individuals interpret the world. By striking a balance between scientific inquiry and religious understanding, societies can cultivate informed, open-minded citizens who are capable of engaging with complex global challenges.

References

9. Eickelman, D. F. (1992). The Middle East and Central Asia: An Anthropological Approach. Prentice Hall.

10. Forrest, B., & Gross, P. R. (2007). *Creationism's Trojan Horse: The Wedge of Intelligent Design*. Oxford University Press.

11. Jegede, A. S. (2007). "What Led to the Nigerian Boycott of the Polio Vaccination Campaign?" *PLoS Medicine*, 4(3), e73.

12. Pew Research Center. (2019). *A Changing World: Global Views on Climate Change and Education Levels.* Retrieved from www.pewresearch.org.

4.2. Cultural and Societal Influences:

Education is often regarded as the foundation of a progressive society, enabling individuals to develop critical thinking, problem-solving abilities, and informed decision-making skills. However, education systems are not isolated from societal forces. Cultural traditions, religious beliefs, political ideologies, and technological advancements all play crucial roles in shaping how education is structured and delivered. In some cases, these influences foster intellectual growth, while in others, they serve as tools for manipulation and control.

In many parts of the world, religious ideologies continue to influence curricula, sometimes at the cost of scientific knowledge. Similarly, political systems shape educational policies, often prioritizing ideological loyalty over academic excellence. The role of media and technology in disseminating both knowledge and misinformation further complicates this landscape. In some cases, governments intentionally weaken education to maintain control over citizens, ensuring they remain dependent on religious or political authority.

This raises an important question: Is education being used to empower individuals or as a means to control them?

4.2.1. Balancing Science and Religion: A Cultural Dilemma

Throughout history, societies have struggled to reconcile scientific discoveries with religious doctrines. While some have successfully integrated both, others have resisted scientific progress to maintain religious authority. One of the most well-known historical examples is the Catholic Church's condemnation of Galileo Galilei in the 17th century for supporting heliocentrism—the idea that the Earth revolves around the sun. The Church saw this as a direct challenge to its teachings, leading to Galileo's persecution (Drake, 1978). Similar conflicts persist today in many parts of the world. In the United States, there have been repeated efforts by religious groups to challenge the teaching of evolution in public schools. Some states have pushed for "intelligent design" to be included in science curricula despite overwhelming scientific evidence supporting evolution (Branch & Scott, 2009).

In Turkey, the government removed evolution from school curricula in 2017, citing its "controversial" nature (Rousseau, 2017). Saudi Arabia's education system, similarly, prioritizes Islamic theology over scientific inquiry (Doumato, 2003). These examples illustrate how religious ideologies shape education policies, often limiting students' exposure to scientific reasoning. However, some societies have successfully balanced science and religion. Japan, for example, maintains a strong emphasis on technological advancement while preserving its cultural and religious traditions. Scandinavian countries prioritize scientific literacy while respecting religious freedoms, fostering an environment where critical thinking is encouraged.

The extent to which science and religion coexist in education depends on cultural attitudes toward knowledge. While some societies promote inquiry and progress, others suppress it, often stunting intellectual and technological advancement in the process.

4.3. The Role of Politics, Media and Technology in Shaping Perceptions

Beyond religion, political systems, media, and technology play significant roles in shaping education. Governments often manipulate curricula to serve ideological purposes, sometimes deliberately weakening education to maintain control over citizens.

4.3.1. Political Manipulation of Education

Authoritarian regimes throughout history have used education as a tool for propaganda. Nazi Germany, for example, rewrote textbooks to glorify Aryan supremacy and spread anti-Semitic ideology, shaping young minds into loyal Nazi followers (Evans, 2005). The Taliban's rule in Afghanistan severely restricted education for women, ensuring that half the population remained economically and socially dependent on men (Rahimi & Lisosky, 2016).

A more contemporary example is India, where government spending on religious events has skyrocketed while investment in education has stagnated. Large-scale religious gatherings such as the Kumbh Mela and the construction of grand temples receive massive state funding, while government schools suffer from neglect. According to the **Union Budget 2023-24**, the Indian government allocated **₹2,300 crore** ($280 million) for the promotion of religious tourism and temple construction, while the education sector saw only a **5% increase**—insufficient to address the growing crisis of school closures (MHRD, 2023).

As a result, many government schools in rural India have shut down due to lack of funds, forcing children from poor families out of the education system. Private schools, which remain operational, are often too expensive for economically disadvantaged families. The declining investment in education ensures that a significant portion of the population remains uneducated, preventing them from developing critical thinking skills that could challenge the status quo.

4.3.2. Media and the Spread of Misinformation

In today's digital era, media and technology have become powerful forces in shaping public perceptions of education. While the internet provides access to vast amounts of information, it also facilitates the spread of misinformation. This is particularly evident in the rise of pseudoscience and conspiracy theories that undermine scientific education.

For example, during the COVID-19 pandemic, misinformation about vaccines spread rapidly across social media platforms. Religious and political groups opposing vaccinations propagated false claims that vaccines were unsafe, despite scientific evidence proving otherwise. This led to vaccine hesitancy, demonstrating how media can manipulate public perception and hinder scientific progress (Ball, 2021).

Additionally, social media algorithms prioritize sensational content over factual accuracy, creating echo chambers where misinformation thrives. In many countries, students rely on digital platforms for information, making them vulnerable to biased narratives that reinforce political or religious agendas. This underscores the need for media literacy education to equip students with the skills to critically evaluate information sources.

4.3.3. The Consequences of Neglecting Education

The consequences of neglecting education in favor of religious and political agendas are profound and long-lasting. When a society fails to prioritize education, it experiences slow economic growth due to an unskilled workforce, resulting in high unemployment and limited progress. Additionally, social inequality deepens as quality education becomes accessible only to the wealthy, restricting social mobility and widening the gap between different economic classes. A lack of education also makes populations more vulnerable to fundamentalist ideologies, increasing societal divisions and fostering extremism. Furthermore, democracy weakens when citizens are deprived of education, as critical thinking and informed decision-making decline, making people more susceptible to propaganda and authoritarian rule. India's current situation, where religious events receive significant funding while many schools face closures due to inadequate support, serves as a stark warning. A society that values religious spectacle over intellectual development risks stagnation, rising inequality, and diminished global competitiveness, ultimately jeopardizing its future growth and stability.

Education remains one of the most powerful tools for societal progress. However, its effectiveness depends on how it is shaped by cultural, religious, political, and technological influences. Some societies embrace scientific inquiry, fostering an environment of innovation and critical thinking. Others, driven by religious dogma or political control, weaken education systems to maintain ideological dominance.

India's declining investment in education, coupled with increased spending on religious events, exemplifies how governments manipulate public priorities to serve political interests. Unless urgent reforms are made, the country risks creating a generation of undereducated citizens unable to compete in a globalized world.

Ultimately, the question remains: Will education be used to empower individuals with knowledge and reasoning skills, or will it be exploited as a tool to perpetuate ignorance and control? The answer lies in the choices societies make today.

References

- Ball, P. (2021). "The Lightning-Fast Spread of COVID Misinformation." *Nature*, 589(7843), 322-324.
- Branch, G., & Scott, E. (2009). "The Latest Face of Creationism in the United States." *Science*, 322(5908), 1622-1623.
- Doumato, E. A. (2003). "Manning the Barricades: Islam According to Saudi Arabia's School Texts." *The Middle East Journal*, 57(2), 230-247.
- Drake, S. (1978). *Galileo at Work: His Scientific Biography*. University of Chicago Press.
- Evans, R. J. (2005). *The Third Reich in Power*. Penguin Books.
- Ministry of Human Resource Development (MHRD), India. (2023). "Union Budget 2023-24: Education Sector Analysis."
- Nair, R. (2018). "Textbook Revisions and the Politics of History in India." *Economic and Political Weekly*, 53(2), 12-15.

- Rahimi, B., & Lisosky, J. M. (2016). *Media and Gender in Afghanistan*. Bloomsbury Publishing.
- Rousseau, S. (2017). "Turkey's Evolution Ban: A Step Backward for Science Education." *Science*, 357(6346), 756-757.

Chapter V

Bridging the Divide

5.1. Harmony Between Science and Religion:

5.1.1. Bridging the Divide: Harmony Between Science and Religion

Science and religion have often been perceived as conflicting forces, with science relying on empirical evidence and rationality, while religion is rooted in faith and spiritual experiences. However, history and contemporary discourse reveal a more nuanced relationship, where these domains not only coexist but can complement each other in understanding the universe and human existence. While tensions have existed, many prominent thinkers, both in the past and present, have demonstrated that scientific inquiry and religious belief are not mutually exclusive but can enrich each other in meaningful ways.

5.1.2. Scientists Who Are Religious and Religious Figures Who Embrace Science

Throughout history, numerous scientists have upheld religious beliefs while making groundbreaking scientific discoveries. One prominent example is **Sir Isaac Newton (1643–1727)**, a devout Christian who saw his scientific work as a means to understand God's creation. Newton's laws of motion and universal gravitation laid the foundation of classical physics, yet he also wrote extensively on biblical prophecies and theology. He believed that natural laws were a reflection of divine order and saw no contradiction between faith and reason.

Another significant figure is **Gregor Mendel (1822–1884)**, an Augustinian monk whose experiments with pea plants established the principles of heredity, forming the basis of modern genetics. Mendel's work exemplifies how religious life and scientific inquiry can intertwine harmoniously. His discoveries in genetics were not driven by a desire to challenge religious doctrine but rather to understand the natural order, which he perceived as a manifestation of divine wisdom.

In the contemporary era, **Francis Collins**, a geneticist and former director of the National Institutes of Health, is an outspoken Christian who led the Human Genome Project. Collins views his faith and scientific work as mutually enriching, stating in his book *The Language of God* (2006) that DNA is "the language in which God created life." He argues that understanding the human genome only deepens his sense of wonder and belief in a higher power.

Similarly, religious leaders have embraced scientific discoveries and advancements. **Pope John Paul II**, in a 1996 address to the Pontifical Academy of Sciences, acknowledged evolution as "more than a hypothesis," demonstrating the Catholic Church's openness to scientific perspectives. His statement signified a significant shift in the Catholic Church's stance on scientific theories that were once seen as conflicting with religious doctrine. Likewise, the **Dalai Lama** has expressed great interest in neuroscience and the study of consciousness, advocating for a dialogue between Buddhist philosophy and modern science. He has collaborated with scientists to explore the intersections between meditation, mental well-being, and neurological health, showing how religious practices can benefit from scientific research.

Other religious figures who have embraced science include **Georges Lemaître (1894–1966)**, a Belgian priest and physicist who proposed what later became known as the **Big Bang Theory**. Lemaître's work illustrates that religious conviction does not necessarily preclude scientific exploration. In fact, he viewed the origin of the universe as a moment of divine creation, aligning both scientific inquiry and theological reflection.

5.1.3 The Concept of "Non-Overlapping Magisteria"

The late evolutionary biologist **Stephen Jay Gould** proposed the concept of "Non-Overlapping Magisteria" (NOMA) in his book *Rocks of Ages* (1999). According to Gould, science and religion represent separate domains of teaching authority—science explains the natural world based on empirical evidence, while religion addresses moral values and spiritual meaning. This framework suggests that science and religion need not be in conflict but can coexist by focusing on their respective realms.

An example illustrating NOMA is the Catholic Church's stance on the Big Bang theory. In 1951, **Pope Pius XII** acknowledged the Big Bang as a plausible explanation for the origin of the universe, without negating the role of divine creation. This demonstrates how religious institutions can integrate scientific discoveries into their theological frameworks without rejecting faith.

Moreover, Islamic scholars during the **Golden Age of Science (8th–14th centuries)** made substantial contributions to mathematics, medicine, and astronomy, viewing their scientific pursuits as a way to understand

God's creation. Figures like **Alhazen (Ibn al-Haytham)**, the father of optics, and **Avicenna (Ibn Sina)**, a pioneering physician, exemplified this synthesis of faith and science. They saw no contradiction between religious devotion and scientific discovery, believing that studying the natural world was a form of worship and a means of comprehending divine wisdom.

5.1.4. The Buddhist Perspective on Science

Buddhism has a long-standing tradition of inquiry and empirical observation, making it uniquely compatible with scientific exploration. The **Dalai Lama** has emphasized the importance of integrating scientific discoveries with Buddhist philosophy, particularly in areas such as neuroscience, psychology, and quantum physics. He has actively participated in dialogues with leading scientists through platforms like the **Mind and Life Institute**, which explores the intersection of Buddhist contemplative practices and modern scientific research.

Buddhist philosophy aligns with scientific methods in its emphasis on direct experience and rational inquiry. The **Kalama Sutta**, a Buddhist scripture, encourages skepticism and independent investigation rather than blind faith. This openness to empirical validation has led to extensive research on meditation and its effects on brain function, with studies showing that mindfulness and meditation can significantly enhance cognitive function, emotional regulation, and overall well-being. Neuroscientists have found that Buddhist meditation techniques contribute to neuroplasticity, reinforcing the idea that spiritual practices can have tangible, measurable effects on the human brain.

Additionally, some Buddhist concepts resonate with modern physics. For example, the idea of **interdependent origination**—that all phenomena arise due to interconnected causes and conditions—finds parallels in quantum mechanics, where particles and forces are deeply interwoven. Some Buddhist scholars and scientists argue that these philosophical insights offer valuable perspectives on the nature of reality and consciousness, fostering a holistic dialogue between science and spirituality.

The perceived divide between science and religion is not an inherent conflict but rather a dynamic interplay that has evolved over time. Many scientists maintain religious beliefs, and many religious leaders support scientific inquiry, demonstrating that these realms can be complementary rather than contradictory. The concept of Non-Overlapping Magisteria provides a useful framework for fostering dialogue between science and faith, enabling a more holistic understanding of existence. Likewise, Buddhist perspectives, with their emphasis on empirical inquiry and the study of consciousness, further illustrate that spiritual traditions can coexist with scientific exploration. Rather than viewing science and religion as opposing forces, recognizing their unique strengths and distinct contributions can lead to greater mutual respect and collaboration in addressing some of humanity's most profound questions.

References

- Collins, F. (2006). *The Language of God: A Scientist Presents Evidence for Belief.* Free Press.
- Gould, S. J. (1999). *Rocks of Ages: Science and Religion in the Fullness of Life.* Ballantine Books.
- John Paul II. (1996). "Message to the Pontifical Academy of Sciences on Evolution."
- Newton, I. (1687). *Philosophiæ Naturalis Principia Mathematica.*

- Pius XII. (1951). "Address to the Pontifical Academy of Sciences on the Big Bang."
- The Dalai Lama. (2005). *The Universe in a Single Atom: The Convergence of Science and Spirituality.* Broadway Books.
- Lemaître, G. (1931). "The Beginning of the World from the Point of View of Quantum Theory." *Nature.*
- Nasr, S. H. (1996). *Science and Civilization in Islam.* Harvard University Press.
- Wallace, B. A. (2009). *Mind in the Balance: Meditation in Science, Buddhism, and Christianity.* Columbia University Press.
- Ricard, M., & Thuan, T. X. (2001). *The Quantum and the Lotus: A Journey to the Frontiers Where Science and Buddhism Meet.* Crown Publishing Group.

5.2. The Future of Science and Religion:

5.2.1. Emerging Trends in Spirituality and Scientific Discovery

The relationship between science and religion has been a topic of debate for centuries. In modern times, the two have taken divergent paths, with science providing empirical explanations for natural phenomena and religion offering spiritual and ethical guidance. However, emerging trends suggest a shift in how spirituality and scientific discovery interact. Today, more individuals embrace a form of spirituality that is compatible with scientific principles, often leaning towards secular humanism or philosophical naturalism. The increasing acceptance of scientific reasoning in traditionally religious societies indicates a gradual move toward evidence-based thinking. For instance, the Vatican Observatory, an astronomical research institution under the Catholic Church, acknowledges the Big Bang theory and evolution, demonstrating how religious organizations are adapting to scientific discoveries rather than resisting them (Coyne, 2015).

Another significant trend is the role of neuroscience in understanding religious experiences. Research on meditation and prayer, using fMRI scans, has revealed that spiritual practices activate certain brain regions associated with emotional regulation and self-awareness (Newberg et al., 2017). This scientific inquiry into spirituality helps differentiate between faith-based beliefs and the physiological effects of religious practices. It also allows individuals to appreciate spirituality without subscribing to supernatural explanations, paving the way for a more rational approach to personal well-being.

5.2.2. How Mental growth Might Evolve in a World Increasingly Shaped by Technology and Globalization

The modern world is rapidly evolving, primarily due to technological advancements and globalization. As artificial intelligence, biotechnology, and space exploration push the boundaries of human understanding, mental growth is also undergoing transformation. The shift towards scientific literacy is a key factor in cognitive evolution, enabling individuals to rely on logic and reason rather than religious dogma. The rise of online education and access to vast amounts of scientific information through the internet has accelerated this transition.

A notable example of this change is the increasing secularization in developed nations. In countries like Sweden and Japan, where science and technology drive progress, religious affiliation has significantly declined.

According to a 2021 Pew Research report, Sweden has one of the lowest rates of religious belief globally, correlating with high scientific literacy and technological development (Pew Research Center, 2021). This trend suggests that as societies become more educated and technologically advanced, religious influence diminishes, allowing for greater intellectual and social progress.

Interestingly, Hindu mythology itself contains wisdom that aligns with scientific principles. Lord Krishna, in the Bhagavad Gita, stated that "The change is the law of nature." This profound statement underscores the inevitability of progress and adaptation. However, the irony remains that many of his followers resist change and cling to outdated traditions and beliefs, often hindering social and intellectual evolution. While ancient scriptures may advocate for growth and transformation, rigid interpretations and dogmatic adherence to rituals prevent society from embracing scientific progress fully.

5.2.3. Science as the Foundation of Human Civilization

Human civilization has thrived due to scientific discoveries rather than religious doctrines. Every major advancement, from medical breakthroughs to space exploration, is a testament to the power of science in shaping the world. Electricity, vaccines, artificial intelligence, and genetic engineering have revolutionized human existence, improving life expectancy, communication, and overall well-being. Religion, on the other hand, has historically imposed restrictions on knowledge and societal growth. The medieval suppression of scientific thought, such as the persecution of Galileo Galilei for advocating heliocentrism, is a prime example of how religious dogma has hindered intellectual progress (Finocchiaro, 2008).

In contrast, when societies prioritize scientific inquiry over religious doctrine, they achieve remarkable progress. Countries that emphasize science and technology, such as South Korea and Germany, have emerged as global leaders in innovation and economic growth. Conversely, regions where religious fundamentalism dictates social policies often experience stagnation in education and human rights. The oppression of women's rights in some conservative religious societies further illustrates how dogmatic beliefs can restrict social progress, whereas scientific reasoning promotes equality and empowerment.

The future of science and religion will likely be defined by a continued divergence, with science playing an increasingly dominant role in shaping human thought and development. While spirituality may persist in various forms, its influence will likely be shaped by empirical understanding rather than traditional religious dogma. For human civilization to continue advancing, embracing science is not just beneficial—it is essential. The more societies prioritize rationality and scientific inquiry over religious constraints, the greater their potential for intellectual and social growth.

References

- Coyne, J. A. (2015). *Faith vs. Fact: Why Science and Religion Are Incompatible.* Viking.
- Finocchiaro, M. A. (2008). *Retrying Galileo, 1633–1992.* University of California Press.
- Newberg, A., D'Aquili, E., & Rause, V. (2017). *Why God Won't Go Away: Brain Science and the Biology of Belief.* Ballantine Books.
- Pew Research Center. (2021). *The Future of World Religions: Population Growth Projections, 2010-2050.* Pew Research Center.

Chapter VI
Conclusion

6.1. Summary of Key Insights:

6.1.1. The Complementary Roles of Science and Religion in Mental growth

Science and religion, often perceived as opposing forces, can work harmoniously to enhance mental growth. Science fosters critical thinking, rationality, and empirical understanding, while religion provides moral guidance, emotional resilience, and a sense of purpose. Together, they contribute to a well-rounded intellectual and spiritual growth, encouraging individuals to explore both the material and metaphysical aspects of existence.

6.1.2. The Importance of Fostering a Balanced Perspective

A balanced perspective, integrating both scientific reasoning and spiritual wisdom, is essential for holistic development. Embracing diverse viewpoints allows individuals to navigate complex life challenges with clarity and wisdom. By acknowledging the strengths of both science and religion, one can cultivate open-mindedness, adaptability, and a deeper appreciation for the interconnectedness of knowledge and belief.

In conclusion, the synergy between science and religion enriches mental growth by providing both analytical tools and ethical frameworks. A balanced perspective ensures a more profound understanding of the world and fosters a harmonious approach to personal growth and societal progress.

6.2. Final Thoughts

Encouraging open-mindedness and fostering dialogue between science and religion is essential for a more enriched and comprehensive understanding of the world. Rather than viewing them as opposing forces, recognizing their complementary nature allows for greater intellectual and spiritual growth. Science provides empirical knowledge and a systematic approach to discovering the universe's mysteries, while religion offers ethical guidance, purpose, and emotional resilience. When both perspectives are engaged in meaningful conversations, individuals can develop a more nuanced worldview that respects both logic and faith.

A more integrated approach to understanding the human experience has the potential to bridge gaps between knowledge and belief, leading to a more holistic way of thinking. By embracing the strengths of both disciplines, individuals can cultivate wisdom, compassion, and a deeper appreciation for life's complexities. This balance can contribute to personal fulfillment, social harmony, and the advancement of human civilization by integrating scientific progress with ethical and philosophical insights. A society that encourages both scientific exploration and spiritual wisdom fosters innovation while maintaining moral integrity.

At the same time, religious individuals must remain vigilant against those who manipulate faith for personal or political gain. Throughout history, various groups have exploited religious sentiments to create division, spread misinformation, or push political agendas that do not align with the core values of spirituality—compassion, justice, and truth. Blind allegiance to such forces can hinder progress and breed intolerance. Therefore, it is crucial for people of faith to critically assess the intentions behind religious and political narratives, rejecting those who use religion as a tool for power rather than as a means of promoting harmony and moral guidance. Byboycotting such exploitative influences and focusing on the true essence of faith, believers can ensure that religion remains a source of unity, wisdom, and ethical progress rather than a mechanism for control and division.

Ultimately, an open and inclusive mindset encourages growth, understanding, and a more profound connection to the world and each other. When individuals approach both science and religion with curiosity and discernment, they can create a future that values truth, fosters peace, and upholds the dignity of all human beings.

....

www.ingramcontent.com/pod-product-compliance
Lightning Source LLC
LaVergne TN
LVHW091110150826
845673LV00002B/774

* 9 7 9 8 8 9 7 4 4 0 1 8 4 *